CW01082721

Original title:

Quantum Love

Author: Kene Elistrand

ISBN HARDBACK: 978-9916-89-244-2

ISBN PAPERBACK: 978-9916-89-245-9

ISBN EBOOK: 978-9916-89-246-6

Celestial Interactions

Stars whisper secrets in the night,
Galaxies twirl in a dance of light.
Constellations map our dreams untold,
While comets rush with stories bold.

Planets align in a cosmic show,
Moonlit tides ebb and flow.
Solar winds carry soft caress,
In this universe, we find our bliss.

Nebulas cradle the seeds of time,
Echoes of old, a celestial rhyme.
Light-years stretch like threads of fate,
Connecting hearts across the cosmic gate.

Asteroids drift, a silent ballet,
While shooting stars make wishes sway.
In the vastness, we seek our place,
Among the wonders of infinite space.

In this dance of celestial fire,
We chase the sparks of our desire.
Hand in hand, we spin and glide,
In the universe, forever side by side.

The Entropy of You and Me

The clock ticks softly, moments fade,
Fragments of us in memories laid.
Chaos swirls in the cups of time,
In the heart's echo, we find our rhyme.

Your laughter dances in the air,
Like fleeting whispers, light as prayer.
Every glance, a universe shifts,
Amidst the shadows, love uplifts.

Yet entropy pulls, threading apart,
As colors bleed from the canvas of heart.
We tread a line of joy and pain,
Underneath the sun and rain.

In disarray, we laugh and cry,
Through tangled paths, we learn to fly.
The beauty lies in every scar,
Mapping the journey of who we are.

Bound by chaos, yet deeply aligned,
In the fabric of fate, our hearts entwined.
Though the world may spin and bend,
With you, my love, there's no end.

The Strings That Bind Us.

In shadows deep, our laughter weaves,
A tapestry of dreams and leaves.
With every thread, our souls entwine,
A bond unbroken, yours and mine.

Through storms we sail, hand in hand,
In silence, we understand.
Each whispered word, a secret shared,
In the fabric of love, we are ensnared.

The universe hums a gentle tune,
As stars align beneath the moon.
With every heartbeat, I feel the pull,
Of strings that bind, so beautiful.

In moments lost, in time's embrace,
We find our way, our sacred space.
No distance great can break the line,
For in my heart, your spirit shines.

Together we weave, through thick and thin,
In the art of love, we find our win.
A dance of hearts, forever free,
The strings that bind, just you and me.

Entanglement in Your Eyes

In the depths of your gaze, I find my home,
A universe where even shadows roam.
With every glance, a spark ignites,
Entangled fates in endless nights.

Your laughter dances in the air,
A melody of truth, beyond compare.
Through veils of doubt and fear we tread,
In the symphony of love, our hearts are led.

As galaxies swirl in cosmic rhyme,
We navigate the fabric of time.
In tangled dreams, we lose control,
Yet find ourselves, heart and soul.

In silence, your essence speaks to me,
A whisper of what's meant to be.
Through every storm, we stay aligned,
In the light of love, two souls combined.

Entangled threads of dark and light,
Draw us closer in the night.
In your eyes, I see the stars,
A love so strong, it knows no bars.

The Dance of Subatomic Hearts

Beneath the veil of what we see,
Are hearts that pulse in harmony.
In cosmic waltz, with grace we twine,
A dance of particles, yours and mine.

Amidst the chaos, we find our beat,
In rhythm soft, our spirits meet.
The universe spins, with every glance,
In quantum realms, we take our chance.

With every touch, the world ignites,
An explosion of dreams in tranquil nights.
In this vast space, our energies flow,
The dance of hearts, an endless show.

Through every twist and turn, we sway,
In the language of love, we find our way.
No boundaries hold, no limits confine,
In the subatomic, our hearts align.

Together we leap, through shadows bright,
In the dance of life, we find our light.
An intricate ballet, soft and profound,
Where love is the force in every sound.

Infinite Echoes of Us

In whispers soft, I hear your name,
An echo bound in love's sweet flame.
With every moment, a memory grows,
In infinite echoes, our spirit flows.

Across the canvas of time and space,
We paint our dreams, a sacred place.
Through laughter's ring and sorrow's sigh,
In echoes of us, we'll never die.

The universe hums our timeless song,
A melody that binds us strong.
With every beat, our hearts collide,
In infinite echoes, you're by my side.

Through peaks and valleys, loud and clear,
The sound of love is always near.
In the silence and in the rush,
Infinite echoes, a gentle hush.

So let us dance in the cosmic sway,
In echoes of us, come what may.
For in this life, our love will guide,
An infinite journey, heart open wide.

Fragments of Celestial Togetherness

In the whispers of the night,
Stars twinkle soft and bright.
A dance of dreams in the sky,
Where souls meet and never die.

Time flows like a gentle stream,
Woven hearts share one pure dream.
Fragments of light in embrace,
Together they find their place.

Underneath the moon's soft glow,
Radiant bonds that ebb and flow.
Each moment glimmers and fades,
In this cosmic serenade.

Galaxies spin, worlds align,
Searching for a sign, divine.
In this vastness, hand in hand,
Together we make our stand.

Eons pass like fleeting dust,
Yet in our bond, we find trust.
Across the void, love persists,
In celestial twilight's mist.

Cosmic Threads of Destiny

Weaving tales in starlit skies,
Each thread whispers, never lies.
Across the cosmos, fates entwine,
In every heartbeat, yours and mine.

A dance beneath the silver veil,
Guided by the stars' sweet trail.
Each moment stitched, forever bright,
Creating paths of pure delight.

Destiny calls in sacred tones,
Merging spirits, hearts, and bones.
In the tapestry of night,
We find our love, our shared light.

Through shadows cast by worlds unknown,
Together in this space we've grown.
Threads of time that stretch and span,
Binding us, woman and man.

Glimmers of hope in distant dreams,
Life unfolds in vivid seams.
Cosmic threads that brightly weave,
In each other, we believe.

Entangled Frequencies

In the hum of the universe,
Frequencies speak, a sweet converse.
Entangled souls in sync we find,
A harmony of hearts and mind.

Echoes dance through time and space,
Vibrations warm, a soft embrace.
Together, we move like the tide,
In each beat, love won't divide.

Resonating with gentle light,
Each pulse a promise shining bright.
Whispers of fate through midnight air,
In every note, we are aware.

Crashing waves against the shore,
Entangled in rhythms, we explore.
With each heartbeat, we create,
A symphony that won't abate.

In every silence, voices blend,
Entangled frequencies, no end.
In this cosmic symphony,
Together, we will always be.

Vortex of Emotions

In the whirl of feelings deep,
A vortex draws our hearts to leap.
Tides of joy, waves of despair,
In this storm, our hopes lay bare.

Around us, passions twist and sway,
Colors clash in bold array.
Emotions flow like rivers wide,
In each current, we collide.

The eye of calm in chaos swirls,
In love's embrace, the tempest twirls.
Through every rise and every fall,
We stand together, through it all.

Amid the noise, we find our song,
In the rapture, we belong.
Holding tight, we brave the night,
In this vortex, we ignite.

Love, a force that breaks the chains,
In the whirlwind, joy remains.
Through every storm, we'll find a way,
Creating light from shades of gray.

Fractal Whispers in the Cosmos

Stars twinkle softly in the night,
Patterns unfurl, a cosmic sight.
Galaxies spin, a dance so grand,
Fractal whispers across the land.

Celestial echoes softly play,
As colors blend in night's ballet.
In the spiral arms of delight,
We find our place, our hearts take flight.

Nebulas bloom in twilight's grace,
Every spark, a whispered trace.
The universe sings, vibrant and wild,
In the depths of dreams, we're reconciled.

Every heartbeat echoes, a song,
In cosmic threads, we all belong.
From the void, our spirits rise,
Fractal whispers, endless skies.

In the silence, we feel the spark,
Guided by starlight in the dark.
With the cosmos, we twist and twine,
In infinite realms, your hand in mine.

Parallel Universes of Desire

In the shadows of the night,
Parallel worlds come to light.
Each desire, a path unknown,
Mirrored hearts, yet all alone.

Choices made in whispered breath,
Each a dance, a flirt with death.
In the depths of dreams, we roam,
Searching figures that feel like home.

Time unwinds, the fabric bends,
On this journey, love transcends.
Every pulse, a chance to find,
Another you, a soul entwined.

Fate's hand shapes the skies we see,
In every wish, possibility.
Two hearts beat in cosmic embrace,
Beneath the vast, unending space.

With each moment, lifetimes blend,
Parallel paths that twist and bend.
Though worlds apart, we feel the fire,
Lost in our parallel desire.

The String Theory of Affection

In a world of strings, we play,
Vibrations guide us on our way.
Every note a gentle touch,
Echoing feelings that mean so much.

Like symphonies woven in air,
Our hearts intertwine, a tender snare.
With every pull, a spark ignites,
In the silence, pure delight.

Underneath the cosmic weave,
In each glance, we choose to believe.
Love's resonance rings so clear,
In the fabric of us, I feel you near.

Through dimensions, we softly glide,
In this tapestry, we confide.
Each heartbeat strummed through time's song,
In string theory, we both belong.

In every thread, the truth we find,
Affection holds us, intertwined.
Bound by love, we dance anew,
In this universe, it's me and you.

Beyond the Event Horizon of Touch

Within the void where shadows lie,
We reach for stars in the night sky.
Beyond the edge where silence swells,
A touch that breaks the cosmic spells.

Gravity pulls us, fierce and real,
In this moment, hearts can feel.
A brush of hands ignites the flame,
In the dark, we speak your name.

Time suspends in tender bliss,
Every moment a stolen kiss.
Beyond the event horizon's seam,
We find connection in the dream.

Lost in the depths, a love untamed,
In chaos, our spirits are claimed.
Through the vastness, we dare to leap,
In the shadows, our secrets keep.

Close your eyes, take my hand tight,
Together we burst through the night.
Beyond the event horizon's clutch,
We are forever, in every touch.

The Wave-Particle Duel of Desire

In shadows twist the thoughts we share,
A dance of longing fills the air.
Particles collide, sparks ignite,
In silence deep, we seek the light.

Each glance a wave, the pull is real,
In currents strong, our hearts do feel.
The realms of science, art, collide,
In every pulse, our dreams abide.

As time unfolds, what path is right?
A duel of wishes, day and night.
In every breath, a change of tide,
Together, still, we cannot hide.

Love's Hidden Dimensions

In layers deep, our hearts reside,
A universe where dreams abide.
Through tangled threads of fate we weave,
In quiet moments, we believe.

Dimensions shift, our souls entwine,
In every glance, a secret sign.
We chase the echoes, soft and clear,
In hidden realms, we shed our fear.

Through time and space, our love expands,
In whispered dreams, we make our plans.
A tapestry of hopes and sighs,
In endless worlds, our passion flies.

Celestial Orbits of Longing

Through galaxies, our spirits soar,
In cosmic paths, we seek for more.
The stars align, your light ignites,
In orbit close, our love excites.

Each moment shared, a shifting tide,
In vaults of night, we cannot hide.
The moon bears witness to our flight,
As planets spin through endless night.

In vastness grand, our voices blend,
Transcending space that has no end.
Together bound, we chase the dawn,
In constellations, we are drawn.

The Interstellar Space Between Us

In silence vast, a void remains,
Yet love persists despite the strains.
Across the stars, my heart does yearn,
For bridges built, for worlds to turn.

Each thought a comet, bright and bold,
In starlit dreams, our stories told.
Through wormholes wide, our paths converge,
In distant echoes, feelings surge.

Between us lie the cosmic seas,
Yet love can sail on endless breeze.
In every heartbeat, closeness found,
Though space may part, our souls are bound.

Echolocation of Affection

In the dark, we find a way,
Voices echo, hearts replay.
Soft whispers in the night,
Guide our minds toward the light.

Through the mist of silent thoughts,
Every pulse, a bond that knots.
Frequencies dance in the air,
Telling secrets, we both share.

Call and answer, like a song,
In this harmony, we belong.
Ears attuned to love's sweet beat,
Two souls in rhythm, pure and neat.

In the space where shadows blend,
Love's echo knows no end.
Vibrations touch like morning dew,
Reflecting all the love we knew.

As we navigate our dreams,
Echolocation softly beams.
With every sound, we drift and sway,
Together in this grand ballet.

Vibration of Two Souls

In the silence, we emit,
A frequency, a gentle hit.
Resonating, side by side,
In each heartbeat, love abides.

Tuning forks of soul and mind,
In your laughter, I will find.
Echoes of a distant past,
In this moment, love can last.

Vibrations weave a tender thread,
Binding all the words unsaid.
Every glance, a silent plea,
Two souls dance in harmony.

As the world fades into gray,
Your embrace lights up my way.
Caught in a magnetic pull,
Together, we become so full.

In this space of pure delight,
We're the stars that shine at night.
With every note, with every sigh,
In this vibration, we will fly.

Time's Paradox of Togetherness

In a clock that ticks so slow,
Time stands still when love does grow.
Each second, a fleeting glance,
Caught in our sweet, timeless dance.

Yet moments rush like rivers flow,
Always moving, never slow.
But in your arms, I am found,
Time is lost, forever bound.

Past and future intertwine,
In your eyes, bright stars align.
Every heartbeat marks the way,
Guiding us through night and day.

As hours fade, we hold on tight,
Each minute feels like pure delight.
Against the tide, we swim anew,
In paradox, I cherish you.

So let the moments rush or crawl,
In your essence, I have it all.
Together, let eternity reign,
In love's embrace, we feel no pain.

The Fabric of Emotion

Woven threads of joy and pain,
In every stitch, love's sweet refrain.
Colors blend and shapes collide,
In this tapestry, we abide.

Each emotion, a careful thread,
From laughter shared to tears we shed.
Textures rich with tales to tell,
In our hearts, they weave so well.

Patterns change, but still they tie,
In the fabric, you and I.
With every pull, a bond is spun,
Strengthened more as time has run.

Frayed edges show the life we've led,
Blueprints of dreams we both have fed.
In every corner, love unfolds,
Creating warmth, defying cold.

So let us stitch with gentle hands,
Together, weaving all life's plans.
In this art, our love will grow,
The fabric of emotion's glow.

Portals of Love

In shadows deep, our whispers grow,
Each glance a spark, a gentle glow.
Through secret doors, our souls entwine,
In quiet nights, your heart is mine.

With every touch, the world feels new,
Our laughter dances, skies turn blue.
In tender dreams, we find our place,
Lost in the magic of your embrace.

A garden blooms where fondness thrives,
In every heartbeat, love survives.
The starlit path we walk tonight,
Guided by love's soft, radiant light.

Through portals vast, our spirits soar,
In realms unknown, we still explore.
Together, we are wild and free,
Bound only by love's sweet decree.

So let us weave this tale of grace,
With every step, we'll leave a trace.
In portals bright, our journey starts,
Forever linked, two beating hearts.

Entangled Hearts Across Space

Across the stars, our hearts align,
In cosmic dance, your hand in mine.
The universe breathes, so vast, so wide,
Through every void, our love's a guide.

In quiet moments, time stands still,
Each heartbeat whispers, a gentle thrill.
Galaxies spin, yet here we are,
Entangled souls, the brightest star.

As comets trail in moonlit skies,
We find our truth in boundless ties.
Through every space, we chase the light,
Bound together, love's pure flight.

In darkened nights, your spark remains,
A radiant glow that breaks the chains.
Across the cosmos, love transcends,
Two hearts entwined, the joy never ends.

So let us journey, hand in hand,
Through distant worlds, side by side we stand.
Entangled hearts, a force so rare,
In every breath, a universe to share.

Dimensions of Affection

In layers deep, our feelings grow,
Through shifting sands, we ebb and flow.
Dimensions shift, yet love remains,
A timeless bond that knows no chains.

Each smile a light, each laugh a spark,
Guide us softly through the dark.
In every realm, where shadows play,
Your heart, my compass, lights the way.

In whispers shared, our truths expand,
Across the void, you take my hand.
In every touch, a universe,
The depths of love, our shared converse.

With every heartbeat, worlds collide,
In endless dance, we turn the tide.
The fabric sings of what we've found,
In dimensions vast, our love is bound.

So let us wander, seek what's real,
In every moment, joy we'll feel.
For in these realms of vivid dreams,
Our love transcends, or so it seems.

Ripples in the Cosmic Sea

In cosmic waves, our love takes flight,
With every pulse, we steal the night.
Ripples form in the stellar glow,
In depths of space, our spirits flow.

The tide pulls strong, yet here we stay,
Two hearts adrift, we'll find a way.
Through whispers soft, we share the breeze,
In harmony, we sway with ease.

Each moment's echo, a potent prayer,
In this vast sea, we share a stare.
With every heartbeat, the ripples swell,
In ocean's depths, our story tells.

In starlit nights, we drift and dream,
Together, lost in love's soft gleam.
The cosmic sea, a wonder vast,
Our hearts united, future cast.

So let us ride these waves of grace,
In every current, find our place.
For in this universe of mystery,
Your heart is home, my sanctuary.

Celestial Synchronicity

Stars align in silent grace,
Waves of light in cosmic space.
Whispers of the universe call,
Harmony binds us, one and all.

Planets spin in timeless rhyme,
Galaxies dance beyond our time.
In the vastness, we find our place,
Traveling through the void's embrace.

Nebulas swirl in colors bright,
Echoes of dreams ignite the night.
Each heartbeat, a pulse in the sky,
Connected we are, you and I.

Stardust dreams begin to weave,
In every moment, we believe.
Cosmic symphony plays our song,
In the universe, where we belong.

Celestial bodies, infinite flight,
Drawn together, igniting the night.
In this dance of fate, we twirl,
In the cosmos, our hearts unfurl.

The Dance of Electrons

In unseen paths they drift and play,
Dancing shadows in bright display.
Around the nucleus, they twine,
Creating bonds, a grand design.

Charged with energy, they spin,
In a world where sparks begin.
Their ballet shapes both matter and light,
In the depths of the atomic night.

Whispers of forces, strong and weak,
In the silence, secrets speak.
Through currents that flow, we feel the beat,
The rhythm of life in a pulse so sweet.

Every movement, a story told,
In the quantum realm, both fierce and bold.
Electrons dance in vibrant flow,
Unraveling mysteries, we yearn to know.

In this grand theater, unseen yet true,
They interlace, me and you.
A choreography of hearts and minds,
In the dance of electrons, life unwinds.

The Fabric of Affection

Threads of kindness softly sewn,
In every heart, their warmth is known.
Woven tightly, day by day,
In colorful patterns, come what may.

Gentle gestures, a loving touch,
In the moments that mean so much.
Each smile shared, a stitch anew,
A tapestry of me and you.

Through laughter's echo, sorrows fade,
In the fabric of love, we're never afraid.
Stitched in trust, the seams hold fast,
Binding our future, learning from the past.

Seasons change, yet still we weave,
In every thread, hopes we believe.
A quilt of memories, bright and warm,
In the fabric of affection, we transform.

Together we create our own design,
With every heartbeat, our lives entwine.
In this masterpiece of gentle care,
The fabric of love is always there.

In the Orbit of You

Around you, I find my way,
Like the moon to the sun's warm ray.
In your gravity, I feel so light,
Spinning softly, day and night.

With every glance, you pull me near,
In your presence, I've no fear.
Like planets drawn in a cosmic dance,
With each heartbeat, a fleeting chance.

Your laughter's echo, a soothing sound,
In the orbit of you, I'm spellbound.
Guided by your gentle forces,
Together we chart our unique courses.

Through winds of change and tides that sway,
In your orbit, I wish to stay.
Lost in the starlight of your eyes,
In your universe, my spirit flies.

With you, I've found my endless sky,
In this cosmos, just you and I.
Boundless is the space we share,
In the orbit of love, beyond compare.

Parallel Universes of Desire

In shadows cast by choice, we dwell,
Where dreams collide, in silence swell.
A whisper here, a glance afar,
Two worlds entwined, like distant stars.

Our hearts reside in paths unseen,
Each fervent wish, a vibrant sheen.
Fates interlace, like threads of light,
In endless night, we chase our flight.

As cosmic tides pull us apart,
In every ripple, beats a heart.
Longing stretches, tears like rain,
In every universe, love remains.

Through parallel realms, we often roam,
In every echo, we find our home.
Yearning's flame ignites the dark,
Each heartbeat sings, a fervent spark.

In the tapestry of what could be,
We dance in spaces, wild and free.
Parallel dreams weave stories rare,
In every wish, we're always there.

Hearts in a Vacuum

In empty rooms where echoes cling,
Silence looms, a heavy thing.
A heartbeat's pulse, a distant sound,
In vacuums vast, we spin around.

Our thoughts collide in empty space,
Where shadows linger, seek embrace.
In solitude, two souls can fret,
Yet in the quiet, love begets.

Like stars that shine in darkest night,
We yearn for warmth, for shared light.
In the void, our spirits soar,
Hearts whisper truths we can't ignore.

Gravity drags us to the ground,
Yet in our dreams, we're unbound.
In metaphors of love and war,
We traverse the deep, forever more.

So here we stand in the unknown,
In silent voids, yet not alone.
Hearts in a vacuum, fiercely bright,
Together we burn, igniting night.

Gravity of Connection

Like planets drawn in cosmic dance,
Our orbits shift, a fateful chance.
With every pull, each tender glint,
The gravity of love's sweet hint.

In whispers soft, the silence speaks,
Our hearts find strength when one heart seeks.
A force unseen yet ever real,
Binding us close, a sacred seal.

In every touch, a spark ignites,
With starlit eyes, we chase the nights.
We are the moons to each other's suns,
In every heartbeat, a journey runs.

Through cosmic storms and blazing trails,
Our shared pathways tell the tales.
Bound by forces we can't deny,
Gravity holds us, you and I.

So let the universe engage,
As we create our timeless page.
In every moment, we connect,
A force of fate we can't neglect.

Resonance of Souls

In stillness found, our spirits link,
A harmony that makes us think.
In every glance, a world defined,
The resonance of souls aligned.

Like ripples spreading on a lake,
The vibrations dance, the silence breaks.
Through chords of heart, we learn to sing,
In every note, the joy we bring.

Together swaying, side by side,
In waves of love, we'll always glide.
An orchestra of shared delight,
Resonating through day and night.

With every breath, the echoes grow,
In unity, our spirits flow.
Two kindred souls, forever bound,
In the melody of love, we're found.

So let our hearts compose the song,
In every note, we both belong.
The resonance of souls so pure,
In this connection, we endure.

Entangled Hearts

In shadows deep, our whispers soar,
Two souls collide, forevermore.
With every glance, a silent vow,
In tangled dreams, we find our how.

Bound by threads of silver light,
We navigate the endless night.
Your pulse aligns with mine so near,
In every heartbeat, love is clear.

Through storms and calm, we drift as one,
The journey vast, but never done.
In laughter shared, and tears that flow,
Entangled hearts, we come to know.

With every breath, our fates entwined,
In cosmic dance, our stars aligned.
In every moment, love's decree,
Together, love, just you and me.

So let the world spin wild and free,
For in our hearts, we hold the key.
To navigate this life we chart,
Forever joined, entangled heart.

Waves of Affection

The ocean sings a lullaby,
As waves of love roll gently by.
Each ripple holds a sweet caress,
In currents deep, we find our rest.

The moonlight dances on the sea,
Reflecting dreams, just you and me.
With every splash, our spirits rise,
In salty air, our love defies.

From shore to shore, our hearts embrace,
In tides of time, we find our place.
With every storm, and every calm,
You are the anchor, you are the balm.

Together, we will brave the deep,
With whispered secrets we will keep.
The waves may crash, the winds may wail,
But in our hearts, love will prevail.

So ride the surf, embrace the breeze,
In waves of affection, find our ease.
For every wave that comes to shore,
Our love will grow, forevermore.

The Dance of Particles

In quantum realms where shadows play,
The dance of particles leads the way.
In swirling loops of energy bright,
We find the magic lost from sight.

Two atoms spin, a perfect pair,
In cosmic rhythm, unaware.
With every pulse, creation's start,
A universe born from a single heart.

In silent whispers, forces weave,
Through every moment, we believe.
A spark of life, a breath so fine,
In this vast dance, your hand in mine.

A symphony of waves and sound,
In particles, our love is found.
Together bound by unseen ties,
In this grand dance, our spirits rise.

So let us sway through endless space,
In the dance of particles, we trace.
For every step, each twist, each turn,
A deeper understanding we shall learn.

Fragments of Forever

In shards of glass, reflections gleam,
Each fragment tells a different dream.
Scattered pieces, lost yet found,
In vibrant colors, love unbound.

Through every break, a story wakes,
An echoing heart that softly quakes.
With every shard, a memory glows,
In fragments of forever, love grows.

In the mosaic of our days,
We piece together life's bright maze.
Through joy and sorrow, light and shade,
In fragile moments, love is made.

So gather close, these pieces dear,
In chaos, find what we revere.
For in each fragment, truth is clear,
Love's endless journey draws us near.

Together we will shape the art,
From broken pieces, we'll not part.
In fragments of forever, we see,
A beautiful whole, just you and me.

Tidal Forces of Affection

The moon pulls at the sea,
Whispers of love in waves.
A dance of gravity,
Holding hearts in soft embrace.

With each rise and fall,
Emotions ebb and flow.
In gentle tides we sway,
Forever on this shore.

A storm can break the calm,
Yet still we find our way.
Through whirlpools of chaos,
Love anchors us to stay.

Between the stars we glide,
In sync with the universe.
Each heartbeat a pulse,
In cosmic waves we trust.

As the sun greets the dawn,
Casting light on our dreams,
We ride this tidal force,
Together, we are free.

The Uncertainty of Us

In shadows of silence,
Questions flicker like stars.
What lies deep in your gaze?
Are we near or so far?

Each word hangs in the air,
Suspended like a thread.
We dance on the edge,
Fearful of what's ahead.

Moments slip through our hands,
Like sand in an hourglass.
Are we lost in the drift,
Or is love meant to last?

Between laughter and tears,
A fragile balance sways.
In every doubt, a hope,
In every heart, a maze.

Though the path feels unclear,
Step by step we will roam.
With courage, we'll navigate,
Together, we find home.

Photons of Passion

In a beam of bright light,
Desires spark and ignite.
We radiate connection,
Illuminating the night.

Each glance a constellation,
Your smile a cosmic flare.
We're woven into stardust,
In a universe rare.

Moments freeze in the glow,
Time bends in this dance.
Every kiss is a prism,
Reflecting our romance.

With every whispered word,
We burst into brilliance.
An energy unbound,
Transforming our existence.

Through galaxies of dreams,
We explore the unknown.
Together as we soar,
In light, we've overgrown.

Energy Between Worlds

A spark ignites the dark,
Bridging realms far apart.
In each glance, a lighthouse,
Guiding back to the heart.

The frequency of our souls,
Vibrating through the air.
In this cosmic connection,
We find what's true and rare.

Through dimensions of thought,
We leap and explore wide.
An electric embrace,
With no need to hide.

In currents that collide,
We surge and intertwine.
Transforming the silence,
Into a sacred shrine.

As we travel through space,
In harmony, we dwell.
Together, we'll create,
A universe to tell.

Cosmic Entanglement

Stars whisper secrets in the night,
Galaxies dance in endless flight.
Strings of fate twine and twist,
In the cosmos, nothing can be missed.

Every heartbeat echoes far and wide,
In the silence, mysteries reside.
Time flows like a river deep,
In this vast expanse, we gently leap.

Particles pulse with vibrant hue,
Carried by waves, ever anew.
Connections formed beyond our sight,
In the dark, we find our light.

Woven paths of dust and dreams,
Beneath the stars, nothing's as it seems.
In the void, a spark ignites,
Cosmic love, like endless nights.

Together we soar on celestial beams,
Entangled in each other's dreams.
Fates entwined in a celestial dance,
A universe alive with chance.

The Energy of Us

In every glance, an electric spark,
A silent truth ignites the dark.
Two souls merged in vibrant sound,
In every heartbeat, love is found.

Waves of energy flow and collide,
In this moment, we cannot hide.
Unseen bonds that pull us near,
In the chaos, we find our cheer.

Light and shadow in harmony sway,
Guiding us through night and day.
With every touch, a fire ignites,
The energy of us takes flight.

Patterns shift in a cosmic play,
In our presence, dreams will stay.
Together, we create and grow,
Through every challenge, love will flow.

Resonating hearts, a timeless dance,
In the rhythm of life, we take our chance.
The energy of us, a sacred trust,
In love's embrace, we rise from dust.

Torn Between Dimensions

Between the realms, a soft divide,
In shadows deep, our hearts collide.
A pull from worlds both near and far,
Guiding us by a hidden star.

Caught in threads of time and space,
Each twist, each turn, a new embrace.
Two realities dance in focus,
Caught in a dream, we can't oppose this.

Echoes of futures yet untold,
In whispered winds, our hearts unfold.
A glimpse of what we cannot see,
The fabric of all that we could be.

Voices call from distant shores,
In silent nights, our spirits soar.
Torn between what is and seems,
In our hearts, live countless dreams.

Each choice a path, each breath a chance,
In the cosmic tapestry, we find our dance.
Torn between dimensions, we exist,
In the space between, love's gentle mist.

Love's Infinite Potential

In every moment, a seed we plant,
With every breath, our hearts recant.
Love's whispers echo in the air,
In its embrace, we find our care.

Potential lies in every gaze,
In shared laughter, a gentle blaze.
Boundless dreams that dare to soar,
As love unfolds, we want for more.

In the dance of souls, pure delight,
In love's potential, shadows take flight.
Together we weave a vibrant thread,
In this vast world, with feelings spread.

Every challenge faced, we grow,
In love's embrace, through ebb and flow.
An infinite well, a shining light,
In darkest hours, love shines bright.

Through the ages, we shall remain,
In love's embrace, we break the chain.
Infinite potential, our hearts proclaim,
In this cosmic dance, we find our name.

Quantum Hearts Entwined

In shadows where the molecules play,
Two hearts dance in a mysterious sway.
Their rhythm pulses through the night,
Entwined as one in the soft twilight.

Waves of feeling, a gentle stream,
In the quantum realm of a waking dream.
A spark ignites in the silent air,
Each touch whispers secrets laid bare.

Gravity pulls, a cosmic force,
Together they travel a boundless course.
In every glance, a quasar's light,
The universe swells with their shared delight.

Time bends softly around their forms,
As they weather life's tempestuous storms.
In a multiverse where love takes flight,
Their hearts collide in the velvety night.

Lost in the chaos, they find a way,
In the fabric of space, they sway and play.
Two quantum hearts, forever aligned,
In the infinity of love, so divinely entwined.

Dark Matter of Longing

Silent echoes in the vast night sky,
Yearning shadows that flicker and cry.
Fleeting moments, like dust in the void,
A hunger for warmth that's long been destroyed.

In the darkness where secrets reside,
The weight of longing cannot be denied.
Invisible threads pull at the seams,
Binding the heart with unsaid dreams.

Glimmers of hope in the endless dark,
Each whispered wish, a tiny spark.
Searching for light in a cosmic dance,
To break the chains of a lingering trance.

Drifting through space, a soul cries out,
Amidst the silence, filled with doubt.
The heart's ambition forever at play,
In the dark matter, they long to stay.

Between the stars, a love unspoken,
A universe filled with hearts now broken.
Yet in the shadows where shadows reside,
Hope's light flickers, never denied.

Quantum Fluctuations of the Soul

In the realm where particles collide,
Fluctuations echo, like waves on a ride.
Moments of chaos, a dance so divine,
The rhythm of souls, in the cosmic design.

Every heartbeat, a wave of its own,
In the stillness, the seeds are sown.
The spark of a thought, forever will grow,
In the fabric of love, where energies flow.

Eternal whispers weave through the air,
Entangled spirits beyond all compare.
Every glance, a quantum embrace,
In the depths of the heart, they find their place.

The universe breathes, a gentle sigh,
As lovers entwine beneath the vast sky.
In each fluctuation, they find their way,
Guided by love, they dance and sway.

In a world of chance, they take their stand,
Two souls united, hand in hand.
Through cosmic waves and timeless toll,
They revel in quantum fluctuations of the soul.

Schrödinger's Affection

In the box of fate, where love resides,
Two hearts exist where the mystery hides.
Entangled whispers, both near and far,
A paradox beats like a distant star.

The pulse of longing, both here and gone,
In the realm of doubt, love keeps on.
A tender touch, yet so far away,
In Schrödinger's world, both night and day.

Each choice uncovers a hidden brace,
In love's conundrum, they find their place.
Holding on tight, yet letting it go,
A dance of emotions, ebbing and flow.

In the quantum haze, affection breathes,
Promises drift like soft autumn leaves.
With uncertainty, their hearts align,
In the riddle of love, all is divine.

Together they venture, no map to guide,
Through the realms of chance, they reside.
In the paradox, they find their song,
Schrödinger's affection, where they belong.

Fluctuations of Longing

In the quiet night, I wait,
For whispers soft, a subtle fate.
Dreams drift by, like shadows cast,
Yearning for moments, love unsurpassed.

Time ebbs and flows, a restless tide,
Emotions rise, then try to hide.
A flickering flame, burning bright,
Fears and hopes entwined in flight.

The heart beats loud, yet silence speaks,
In every glance, longing peaks.
Through the void, I chase the trace,
Of what was lost—a warm embrace.

Memories dance in twilight's glow,
In every corner, feelings grow.
A symphony of joy and pain,
Ebbing like the sweet summer rain.

Yet through the storms, I still believe,
In the power of love to weave.
Connections strong, though miles apart,
Forever echo in my heart.

Unified Field of Hearts

In the vast expanse of night,
Two souls meet, in shared light.
Whispers flow, a timeless grace,
Bound together, in this space.

Fingers touch, a spark ignites,
A universe in shared sights.
Every heartbeat sings a song,
In this dance, where we belong.

Across the stars, our dreams collide,
In harmony, we choose to bide.
An endless bond, so deep and true,
In every breath, I find you too.

Through rivers wide, through valleys deep,
Promises made, forever keep.
In the chaos, we find our way,
Unified, come what may.

Together we weave a tapestry,
Of moments rich, of ecstasy.
In the heartbeat of our love,
We soar together, high above.

The Heisenberg Uncertainty of Us

In the quantum realm of our embrace,
Uncertainty dances, time and space.
A fragile balance, a subtle force,
In shadows bright, we chart our course.

Every glance, a measured risk,
In the matrix of love, we exist.
Particles collide, merging dreams,
In the silence, a truth redeems.

The more I seek, the less I find,
In the depths of our entwined mind.
A paradox, this love we weave,
In uncertainty, I believe.

With every theory, new paths arise,
Mysteries unfold under starlit skies.
In the unknown, we find our place,
In the haze of longing, we trace.

Together we float, in endless night,
A tapestry spun from dark and light.
Through the universe, hand in hand,
In the chaos, together we stand.

Love Beyond Measure

In every heartbeat, love expands,
A tapestry woven by gentle hands.
Beyond the stars, beyond the skies,
In whispers soft, our spirits rise.

We wander through the ages, lost,
In every step, we count the cost.
Yet love's embrace, a boundless sea,
In every glance, eternity.

No metric holds what we can feel,
In gentle moments, time is real.
Transcending space, a sacred thread,
A bond that clings, where hearts are led.

Through trials faced, through joys we share,
Love's measurement, beyond compare.
In laughter's echo, in tears that fall,
Together we rise, together we call.

So let the world try to confine,
The depth of love, so pure, divine.
For in this dance of life and fate,
Love beyond measure, we create.

Chaos Theory of Us

In the storm of life we sway,
Paths intertwine, then drift away.
Yet amidst the wild and loud,
We find our peace, a hidden crowd.

Whispers dance in tangled threads,
Where every choice, a garden spreads.
In chaos, patterns start to bloom,
Creating colors, dispelling gloom.

Moments clash, collide, and spin,
From disarray, we rise, begin.
In frayed edges, love's embrace,
Chaos bends, reveals our grace.

We're fractals in this grand design,
Each heartbeat forms a perfect line.
Uncertainty, our faithful friend,
In every turn, we twist and mend.

Through turbulence, we navigate,
Reaching out to love, innate.
In every chaos, find the trust,
Together we create, we must.

The Heisenberg Principle of Trust

In every glance, uncertainty,
What we hold is not what we see.
Trust teeters on shaky ground,
In the silence, truth is found.

Every promise, a wave, a tide,
What's believed, we cannot decide.
Familiar faces shift and change,
In the haze, trust feels strange.

Moments flicker in and out,
What's known drapes heavy doubt.
Yet in faith, we find a way,
To navigate the pull of gray.

Together in this blurry scope,
We weave a fragile thread of hope.
What's measured bends with time and fate,
In our hearts, we learn to wait.

In shared secrets, the truth is bright,
Within shadows, we find our light.
Trust is the dance of knowing less,
In the unknown, we find our best.

Love's Quantum Leap

In a world of distance and chance,
We take the leap, we choose to dance.
Entwined souls in the cosmic sea,
Love unfolds its mystery.

Every heartbeat, a ripple, a wave,
Across the void, the brave and the brave.
In an instant, a spark ignites,
The universe shifts, alters sights.

What's unseen becomes vividly clear,
In the silence, we draw near.
Every touch, a gravitational pull,
In love's embrace, we're never full.

Through quantum states, our hearts collide,
In potential, we cannot hide.
With every leap, we redefine,
The boundaries of yours and mine.

Entangled minds, electrified,
In the dance of love, we abide.
Leap with me into the unknown,
Together, never alone.

Particle Hearts

In the dance of atoms, we align,
Creating bonds, your heart in mine.
Our essence sparks in cosmic glow,
Particles collide, love bestowed.

Every heartbeat, a force unmeasured,
Moments captured, then treasured.
In quantum realms, our spirits soar,
Finding energy at the core.

In wave-like patterns, emotions flow,
Forming tides that ebb and grow.
We're more than just a passing phase,
In this duality, we blaze.

With every smile, we intertwine,
The beauty in chaos, so divine.
Every particle sings a song,
Of love's embrace, where we belong.

In this fusion of light and grace,
We discover our sacred space.
Particle hearts in the universe,
In love's embrace, we immerse.

Fractal Patterns of Passion

In the heart's deep spiral, we entwine,
Colors swirl, emotions align.
Every glance a vivid trace,
A dance of souls in sacred space.

Threads of desire weave and spin,
Infinite circles, where love begins.
Each heartbeat echoes, a rhythmic art,
Fractal patterns of a passionate heart.

Moments glisten like morning dew,
Reflections of me and reflections of you.
In this maze, we lose and find,
The fractals mirror the intertwined.

Through time's lens, we dare to play,
Creating beauty in our stay.
Embers burn and shadows cast,
In our world, forever vast.

Passion's echo through the night,
A never-ending flight of light.
In a spiral's embrace, we explore,
Fractal patterns forever more.

Echoes of a Shared Reality

In whispered dreams, we walk the line,
Colliding worlds, yours and mine.
Echoes linger in the open air,
Moments born from silent prayer.

We share our laughter; we share our tears,
A tapestry woven through the years.
In every heartbeat, the truth we find,
Echoes of a dream, beautifully aligned.

Parallel visions paint the scene,
Where thoughts converge and spaces glean.
Together we navigate the storm,
In a reality where hearts are warm.

Through tangled paths, we forge ahead,
With every step, our fears shed.
In the silence, we hear the sound,
Of shared hearts, forever bound.

In this symphony of souls in flight,
We chase the stars, igniting the night.
Echoes resonate, love's decree,
A shared reality, you and me.

The Singularity of Us

In the void, where time stands still,
Two souls pulsate with fervent will.
A singular point where dreams collide,
In the universe of you and I, we bide.

We are the gravity that bends the light,
The supernova igniting the night.
In every breath, in every sigh,
The singularity of us, you and I.

Through infinite realms, we journey wide,
In mind and matter, we coincide.
Each thought a ripple, each word a spark,
Together igniting the shadows dark.

Connected threads in cosmic dance,
In every glance, a fleeting chance.
The essence of love transcends the fuss,
In the vastness, the singularity of us.

As we traverse the astral sea,
You are the light that guides me free.
In this universe, our essence stays,
The singularity of us, our love's blaze.

Dreamscapes of Entangled Minds

In the twilight of our shared dreams,
Reality fades; nothing's as it seems.
We float on clouds, where thoughts ignite,
Entangled minds in the velvet night.

Painted skies with colors bright,
In this realm, we take flight.
A tapestry woven with threads of fate,
In the dreamscape, we resonate.

Voices whisper secrets untold,
In a dance of spirits, bold and gold.
Every heartbeat a vivid pitch,
In the dreamscape, we find our niche.

Time dissolves, and space expands,
As we wander through unseen lands.
In our minds, we dream and find,
The beauty of entangled minds.

Through starlit paths, we explore and glide,
In this sanctuary, we cannot hide.
Together forever, intertwined,
In the dreamscape of our entangled minds.

The Supernova of Our Connection

In the dark, your light shines bright,
A cosmic dance, two hearts ignite.
Across the void, we find our way,
A supernova brightens our day.

Gravity pulls, we can't resist,
An endless pull, a cosmic twist.
Together we burst, colors unfold,
The universe whispers, secrets told.

In this vast space, we carve our mark,
Two souls entwined, igniting the spark.
Each heartbeat echoes a timeless song,
In this creation, we both belong.

Through stardust trails, we roam so free,
An explosion of love, just you and me.
Over galaxies, our dreams take flight,
In this connection, we are the light.

With every glance, we shine anew,
As constellations tell of me and you.
In this dance of time, we'll always be,
A supernova for eternity.

Entangled Destinies

In a world woven with threads of fate,
We meet at crossroads, never too late.
Two paths align, with stories shared,
In this journey, we both declared.

With every choice, a bond grows tight,
Entwined so deeply, we echo the light.
Shared laughter lingers, sorrow too,
In this tapestry, just me and you.

Through trials faced, we rise and bend,
In this dance of life, we're always friends.
Time may shift, but our hearts will know,
Together we flourish, together we grow.

In woven patterns, our souls are bound,
Every heartbeat whispers, love profound.
As seasons change, and moments test,
We find in each other, the very best.

So let the universe play its tune,
Underneath the stars, beneath the moon.
Together, our destinies intertwine,
In this grand design, you are mine.

The Particle Collision of Passion

In the heart of the cosmos, a spark ignites,
Two particles dance, in shared delights.
With each collision, energy flows,
A surge of passion, the universe knows.

In the lab of hearts, we find the fuse,
As forces collide, we can't refuse.
The warmth of desire, so fierce and bright,
In every embrace, we rewrite the night.

Entangled in chaos, a beautiful mess,
Each moment a whirlwind, nothing less.
Explosive reactions, love's wild embrace,
In every heartbeat, a sacred space.

Through voids we travel, together we wield,
The power of love, our ultimate shield.
In this adventure, we defy all odds,
A particle dance, invoking the gods.

So let the cosmos witness our flame,
In this collision, we'll never be the same.
Together in harmony, we'll always be,
The particle collision of you and me.

Waves of Longing

On shores of silence, our hearts collide,
With tides of longing, we cannot hide.
The moon pulls gently, the ocean sighs,
In every wave, our passion lies.

Each ripple carries, whispers of grace,
In the ocean's arms, we find our place.
With every crash, a promise made,
In the depths of longing, never afraid.

As the waves retreat, they leave behind,
Footprints of love, forever entwined.
Chasing the currents, we dance with the sea,
Waves of desire, so wild and free.

Through storms we weather, in calm we bask,
In the heart of longing, love is our task.
As the sun dips low, we share the dream,
In the waves of longing, we're a seamless stream.

So let the tide rise, let the horizon expand,
In this ocean of love, forever we stand.
For in every wave, our hearts will remain,
Tethered together, through joy and pain.

The Relativity of Touch

In shadows soft our fingers dance,
A fleeting brush, a stolen glance.
The warmth of skin, the pulse of time,
Each heartbeat sings a silent chime.

Distance shrinks in tender space,
Where every touch finds its own place.
Connection felt beyond the skin,
An echo deep where feelings begin.

In whispers low our secrets share,
A world suspended in the air.
The gentle graze ignites the night,
As moments blur in soft twilight.

With every touch, a story told,
Of youth and dreams and hearts so bold.
In fleeting minutes, so they weave,
A tapestry that hearts believe.

So let us linger in this grace,
As time stands still in our embrace.
The relativity we explore,
In every touch, we ask for more.

Singularity of the Heart

In whispered beats, our souls align,
A singular pulse, your heart with mine.
Drawn in a dance, a cosmic thread,
Two lives entwined, where love is fed.

A universe in each embrace,
Two bodies lost in timeless space.
In every glance, a spark ignites,
The echo of our shared delights.

A million stars, yet you're the sun,
In your warmth, my journey's begun.
In shadows deep, we find our light,
In singularity, we take flight.

The harmony of heartbeats play,
In symphony, we drift away.
Together now, we chase the dawn,
In love's embrace, forever drawn.

So let the world fade far from view,
In this embrace, it's me and you.
Through every moment, vast and bright,
In singularity, our hearts take flight.

Correlation of Dream and Reality

In twilight realms where shadows blend,
Our dreams awaken, messages send.
A line that bends, a world anew,
Where every wish ignites the view.

Reality wears a velvet guise,
In whispered hopes, our vision flies.
The fabric weaves both soft and bold,
A tapestry, our fates foretold.

In every thought, a spark ignites,
The dance of dreams in starry nights.
With every breath, the fabric sways,
Between the worlds of night and day.

In echoes soft, reality bends,
Where dreamers walk and time descends.
A fusion rare, our spirits weave,
In every breath, we choose to believe.

So let us wander, hand in hand,
Through worlds of promise, expansive and grand.
In the correlation, seek and find,
The dream of two, forever entwined.

Electromagnetic Attraction

In fields unseen, our hearts collide,
An energy we cannot hide.
Drawn close together, yet apart,
A force of nature, a spark of art.

You are the pull in my deep core,
A gravity I can't ignore.
In every glance, the tension grows,
Wherever you are, my spirit knows.

A dance of ions in the air,
Two souls converge, a lasting flare.
In every moment, the charge ignites,
With every heartbeat, love excites.

An orbit formed, a path defined,
Where thoughts collide and hearts unwind.
In every sigh, the voltage swells,
A story asked, a secret tells.

So let us drift in this embrace,
Together lost in time and space.
In electromagnetic grace,
We find our home, our sacred place.

Cosmic Love Letters

In the silence of the night, we write,
Stardust whispers travel light.
Across galaxies, our essences meet,
Cosmic love, forever sweet.

Through the void, our hearts entwine,
Celestial bodies, yours and mine.
Letters drift on solar winds,
Infinite love, where nothing ends.

Nebulas form our secret space,
Every pulse, a warm embrace.
Planets dance to our gentle tune,
Underneath the watchful moon.

Supernova blooms with our sighs,
In the cosmos, where longing lies.
With every star that brightly gleams,
We fulfill the universe's dreams.

Let's weave our dreams upon the stars,
Light-years traveled, love's memoirs.
In every orbit, I find you there,
Cosmic love, beyond compare.

Transcendence in Every Particle

In every atom, a dance unfolds,
The universe whispers secrets untold.
Transcendent rhythms pulse through time,
Life's essence, in every rhyme.

Particles collide in a vibrant spree,
Creating waves of you and me.
The air electric, with each breath taken,
In moments shared, our spirits awaken.

Gravity tugs as we draw near,
In the void, there's nothing to fear.
The cosmos breathes, within our skin,
Transcendence sings, and love begins.

Light swirls around in a brilliant dance,
We find ourselves lost in the chance.
Time bends, and the world feels new,
In each particle, I see you.

Moments merge like galaxies collide,
In the vastness, we take a ride.
Together always, like the stars above,
Transcendence found, in the heart of love.

The Universe Beneath Your Skin

Your touch ignites a spark divine,
A universe within, designed.
Underneath this fragile shell,
Galaxies twirl, and secrets dwell.

With every heartbeat, stardust flows,
Through veins where ancient magic grows.
Constellations dance behind your eyes,
A vast expanse where wonders rise.

Each smile, a supernova bright,
Illuminating the darkest night.
In the silence, our spirits soar,
Two cosmic souls, forevermore.

Whispers of nebulae fill the air,
Together, we'll travel anywhere.
The universe pulses with our grace,
In every corner, love finds its place.

So let us explore this sacred space,
With every glance, I trace your face.
The universe whispers, deep and true,
A boundless realm, just me and you.

Harmonics of Heartstrings

The heartstrings play a tender tune,
In twilight's glow, beneath the moon.
Echos resonate in gentle waves,
Harmonics cradle, love behaves.

Notes of passion fill the air,
A symphony beyond compare.
Each heartbeat strikes a chord of bliss,
In the spaces, we find a kiss.

Together we compose the night,
Melodies weave, souls take flight.
In the silence, we grasp and hold,
Harmonics of love, forever bold.

Time flows like music, soft and sweet,
With every rhythm, two hearts meet.
A cadence born from dreams we share,
In each moment, we feel the flare.

So let us dance beneath the stars,
Play the notes that heal our scars.
In this orchestra, let love sing,
Harmonics soar on love's bright wing.

Vibrations of Tenderness

In whispers soft, the night unfolds,
A gentle touch, a love that holds.
With every breath, we find our way,
In tender hearts, forever stay.

Through silken dreams, we glide, we sing,
In quiet moments, joy we bring.
A laughter shared, the stars align,
In love's embrace, our spirits shine.

Each heartbeat pulses with sweet grace,
In every glance, a warm embrace.
We dance in rhythm, side by side,
In tender vibrations, we confide.

The world beyond fades from our view,
In sacred space, just me and you.
With every touch, our souls ignite,
In tenderness, we find our light.

The echoes linger, soft and clear,
In quiet moments, you are near.
With open hearts, we rise above,
In timeless peace, we craft our love.

Chaotic Harmony

In swirling storms, chaos finds peace,
A dance of rhythms, never cease.
The clashing notes, a vibrant song,
In discord, beauty finds its throng.

With colors bright and shadows cast,
Each note a journey, ever vast.
A symphony of wild delight,
In chaos born, we find our flight.

The heart beats loud, the soul will sway,
In tangled paths, we lose our way.
Yet in the storm, a voice will rise,
A harmony where chaos lies.

The universe spins, a cosmic play,
In every turn, we drift and sway.
With open arms, embrace the clash,
In chaotic dance, our spirits flash.

In waves of sound, our echoes blend,
From discord's depth, new stories send.
Through trial and strife, we find the tune,
In chaotic harmony, we're in bloom.

The Intersection of Desires

At crossroads where our dreams collide,
In whispered wishes, hearts abide.
Amid the shadows, futures gleam,
In tangled thoughts, we chase the dream.

With open eyes, a world unfolds,
In every heartbeat, stories told.
Desires clash, yet gently blend,
In every struggle, love ascends.

Through winding paths and winding time,
A dance of hope, a silent rhyme.
In flickers bright, our wishes spark,
At intersections, we leave our mark.

With every sigh, new paths arise,
In every tear, a sweet surprise.
Together forged, our dreams ignite,
In desires' depths, we find our light.

The universe bends to our will,
Amidst the chaos, we find still.
At the junction where we align,
In the intersection, hearts entwine.

Dualities Entwined

In shadows cast, the light will creep,
From gentle whispers, secrets seep.
In every clash, a union found,
In dualities, we are unbound.

With passion fierce and tender grace,
In every heartbeat, we embrace.
The yin and yang, a dance so bright,
In dark and light, we take our flight.

Through tender touch and fiery glare,
We weave a tapestry so rare.
In contrasts bold, we harmonize,
In dualities, our spirits rise.

With every struggle, deeper we dive,
In shades of gray, our souls arrive.
Together strong, we find our fate,
In every choice, we celebrate.

The world reflects our inner fight,
In every turn, we find the light.
With hearts entwined, we walk the line,
In dualities, our love will shine.

Emotional Wave Functions

Like tides that ebb and flow,
The heart's rhythms shift and sway.
In currents deep, feelings hide,
Rising and falling, a silent tide.

Oscillations draw us near,
In frequencies we cannot hear.
Our love a wave, both wide and stark,
A dance of light within the dark.

With every crest, a fleeting glance,
The pulse of hope, a sweet romance.
In this vast ocean, we find our way,
Through depths of night and break of day.

In every dip, a lesson learned,
In gentle whispers, passions burned.
Together we ride this endless sea,
Where emotional waves set us free.

From chaos comes a soothing peace,
As wave functions change, our hearts release.
In harmony, our spirits soar,
Caught in the rush, forevermore.

The Gravitational Pull of You

You orbit me like distant stars,
In every glance, pulling from afar.
Your gravity holds my heart so tight,
A force unseen, yet full of light.

With every word, you pull me close,
In your presence, I feel morose.
A celestial dance, a silent fight,
Against the dark, you are my night.

Like planets circling 'round the sun,
In your warmth, I am undone.
Your essence lingers like the moon,
In my universe, you're the tune.

The pull of you, it cannot cease,
In the stillness, I find my peace.
Though we drift through space and time,
Our hearts entwined, a rhythm sublime.

In this cosmos, love's embrace,
An endless journey through time and space.
Your gravitational force, so true,
In every heartbeat, I find you.

Interference Patterns of the Heart

In waves of color, we collide,
Intersecting paths where feelings bide.
A canvas bright, emotions play,
Creating patterns, come what may.

With every touch, a burst of hue,
Your laughter resonates, a chord that's true.
These waves converge, a stunning art,
In the interference of the heart.

Like light that bends in every way,
Our hearts align, dance and sway.
Together we craft a masterpiece,
In this gallery, let love increase.

In moments fleeting, beauty found,
In whispered dreams, our souls are bound.
Each pulse, a brushstroke on the night,
Creating echoes of pure delight.

In this vast frame, feelings ignite,
Through shadows cast, we find our light.
In the interference, we reside,
Two hearts, one wave, forever tied.

Time Dilation of Memories

In the echoes of a fleeting glance,
Time bends softly, lost in chance.
Moments stretch like endless skies,
In the realms of where love lies.

Each laugh a thread, weaving fate,
In golden hours, we captivate.
With every heartbeat, seconds pause,
In the beauty of these silent laws.

Stretched like shadows in the twilight,
Our past collides with the softest light.
In memories held, time starts to sway,
In this transient dance, we find our way.

A tapestry of joy and pain,
In every tear, a sweet refrain.
As seconds linger, we redefine,
In the dilation of love's design.

Through every moment, pure yet fleeting,
Time wraps around our hearts, repeating.
In the depths of remembrance, we soar,
In time's embrace, forevermore.

Superposition of Dreams

In the realm where shadows dance,
Thoughts collide in vivid trance.
Colors swirl, and minds take flight,
Lost in dreams that spark the night.

Fragments weave a tapestry,
Each thread sings of mystery.
Visions pulse like stars aglow,
In the depths where wishes flow.

Whispers echo, soft and deep,
Secrets wrapped in silken sleep.
Fleeting moments intertwine,
In this space, all hearts align.

Layers blend, a cosmic quilt,
A tapestry of hopes distilled.
Reality with dreams embraced,
In this void, we find our place.

Awake to dawn, yet still we yearn,
For the dreams that softly churn.
In the light, the shadows fade,
Yet in dreams, we're unafraid.

Entropy's Embrace

Chaos reigns in whispered sighs,
Stars unravel in night's disguise.
Time cascades like falling leaves,
In its grasp, the heart believes.

Fragments scatter, worlds collide,
In the turmoil, we confide.
Every moment, a fleeting trace,
Lost forever in time's embrace.

Winding paths through tangled fates,
Each decision, fate waits andates.
As we dance in life's grand scheme,
We surrender to the dream.

Harmony in disarray,
Life's sweet chaos leads the way.
In the stillness, we discern,
From the ashes, we will learn.

Embrace the storm, let it flow,
In the tempest, seeds will grow.
For in endings, new paths begin,
In entropy, we find our kin.

The Pulse of a Cosmic Bond

Stars align in silent hymn,
Galaxies twirl, edges trim.
Across the void, our hearts connect,
In the dance, we redirect.

Gravity pulls, a soft caress,
In the cosmos, we find our rest.
Orbits trace a path so bright,
Guided by celestial light.

Each heartbeat echoes through the night,
Waves of energy take flight.
In the vastness, we belong,
A symphony, a timeless song.

Through the whispers of the dawn,
Every moment, a new bond drawn.
In this fabric, you and I,
Linger softly, never shy.

As we gaze at worlds afar,
Feel the pulse of who we are.
Tethered by a cosmic thread,
In this unity, we are led.

Subatomic Whispers

In the heart of matter's dance,
Tiny particles find their chance.
Invisible forces weave and twine,
In the silence, secrets shine.

Quarks and leptons, flickers bright,
In their chaos, pure delight.
Every atom a world contained,
In their essence, truth is gained.

Beyond the surface, realms unfold,
Whispers of the brave and bold.
In the void, where players play,
Time and space begin to sway.

Molecules spin and bond with care,
In this dance, we all share air.
Life emerges from the small,
In their whisper, we find all.

Through the lens, we peer so deep,
In subatomic, secrets keep.
Here in the silence, we will find,
The universe within our mind.

Love in the Multiverse

In a cosmos vast and wide,
Our hearts find paths to collide.
Across the stars, our spirits soar,
Infinite love, forevermore.

In each universe, a spark ignites,
With every glance, the heart takes flight.
Through alternate worlds, hand in hand,
Together we weave a timeless strand.

In realms where colors paint the night,
Your laughter echoes, pure delight.
In every dimension, love remains,
Binding us close through joy and pains.

Parallel dreams, a cosmic dance,
In every heartbeat, a second chance.
With every choice, our bond does grow,
In every lifetime, love's gentle flow.

Through black holes and starlit skies,
Our love transcends, it never lies.
In every variant, we are found,
In this multiverse, we are unbound.

Photon-Kissed Moments

In golden rays the morning beams,
We chase the light, we chase our dreams.
With every smile, a moment gleams,
Photon-kissed, or so it seems.

Beneath the sun, your laughter glows,
In tranquil parks where wild grass grows.
We mingle with time, as joy bestows,
Each second dances, as love flows.

Evening whispers in twilight's glow,
A silken breeze, soft and slow.
Together, we weave memories' show,
In light's embrace, our feelings grow.

With every sunset, colors merge,
A painter's brush where hearts converge.
In every flicker, sweet feelings surge,
Photon-kissed, we feel the urge.

In starlit nights, we find our way,
Under the moon's soft silver ray.
These moments shine, they're here to stay,
In love's embrace, we won't delay.

The Quantum Leap of Us

In spacetime's grip, we boldly leap,
Into the unknown, promises we keep.
With every choice, the future we shape,
The quantum dance of love, escape.

Entangled souls, a tangled fate,
In this vast universe, we navigate.
Through hidden paths, our hearts relate,
In a timeless bond, we celebrate.

Fleeting moments bend and blend,
As physics wanes and love transcends.
In every heartbeat, a message sends,
Through waves of time, our spirit mends.

Possibility blooms with every glance,
In every twist, the stars enhance.
Together we take a daring chance,
Our love a timeless, cosmic trance.

In a world where nothing is sure,
Our connection stands strong and pure.
With echoes of joy that long endure,
In the quantum leap, we find allure.

Entangled Emotions

In tangled threads of heart and mind,
Our feelings dance, beautifully entwined.
With every tear, a lesson learned,
Through stormy nights, our passion burned.

In silence shared, a gentle sway,
Through whispered dreams, we find our way.
With every heartbeat, the truth revealed,
In tangled emotions, our fate is sealed.

Soft laughter plays in quiet rooms,
As sunlight glints through springtime blooms.
In shared moments, our love resumes,
Like fragrant roses that slowly bloom.

In storms we face, together we stand,
With fortitude, we make our plans.
Entangled hearts, we understand,
In every struggle, a love so grand.

Through every twist of fate's cruel game,
In tangled emotions, we stay the same.
With every breath, we feel the flame,
Together, forever, love's sweet name.

Pulsating Atoms of Positivity

In the heart, bright colors bloom,
Radiating light, banishing gloom.
Every beat, a chance to begin,
Filling our souls, igniting within.

With every breath, we find our spark,
Chasing away shadows, lighting the dark.
Hands held tight, we rise and shine,
Together we weave, a world divine.

Laughter dances upon the air,
In moments shared, we shed despair.
Joy like a river, freely flows,
Pulsating atoms, love only grows.

Believe in magic, embrace it true,
In every heartbeat, I find you.
A symphony of hope, we play,
Creating brilliance day by day.

So let us lift each other high,
With positivity, we'll touch the sky.
In the harmony of life, we stand,
Unified and bright, hand in hand.

Quantum Realms of Emotion

In spaces unseen, our feelings twine,
Waves of energy, both yours and mine.
In the quantum dance, we intertwine,
Our hearts pulsate, a rhythm divine.

Light and shadow, forever in play,
Moments collapse, then fade away.
Each thought a particle, a dream set free,
In this vast universe, just you and me.

Echoes of laughter, ripples of pain,
Through tangled thoughts, love will remain.
In these realms where time bends,
Our deepest truths, the heart transcends.

We share a bond that cannot break,
In quantum fields, our spirits wake.
Love like stardust, scattered in flight,
Illuminating the long, dark night.

So let us explore this vast domain,
Where emotions dance, yet hold no chain.
In the silence of space, we will find,
The beauty of being, hearts aligned.

The Cosmic Dance of Lovers

Under starlit skies, our spirits sway,
In a cosmic dance, we find our way.
Galaxies spin, as our hearts ignite,
Twinkling with dreams that burst into light.

With every step, we glide through time,
In the universe's rhythm, we start to rhyme.
Whispers of cosmos wrap us tight,
Guiding our souls into the night.

We leap through space, hand in hand,
Braiding our fates as the universe planned.
In celestial bodies, our love's adorned,
For in every heartbeat, a star is born.

The moon our witness, as shadows play,
In the warmth of starlight, fears fade away.
Together we journey, two hearts as one,
In this cosmic waltz, forever begun.

Let the galaxies witness our embrace,
For in this dance, we find our place.
Forever twirling in love's delight,
In the cosmic dance, we unite.

Entwined in Quantum Fields

In the fabric of space, we softly weave,
Entangled threads of love, hearts believe.
Through fields unseen, our spirits soar,
In limitless realms, we seek for more.

Every whisper, a particle's pulse,
Electrons collide, we feel the rush.
In the depths of silence, energy stirs,
As time flickers by, our essence blurs.

Together we drift, like stars on a stream,
In quantum tides, we chase the dream.
Through swirling dimensions, hand in hand,
In the heart of matter, we understand.

With glimpses of light, our souls intertwine,
Existing in spaces both yours and mine.
A universe vast, yet here we exist,
In the dance of atoms, we persist.

So let our love resonate and swell,
In quantum fields where stories dwell.
With each heartbeat, we redefine,
The beauty found in love's design.

Pulses in the Void

In shadows where whispers dance,
Echoes linger, a fleeting chance.
Stars flicker in the silent night,
Dreams collide, a glimmering light.

Galaxies spin in cosmic grace,
Time stretches in this vast space.
A heartbeat in the endless roam,
Each pulse draws the lost back home.

Nebulas weave their colored threads,
In darkness where imagination treads.
Silence speaks in softest tones,
From chaos, beauty brightly stones.

The void hums a lullaby sweet,
Where every loss becomes complete.
Whispers travel, weaving fate,
In pulses, love and loss await.

Hold tight as the galaxies merge,
In the cosmos where dreams emerge.
Together we navigate the night,
In the pulses of that distant light.

Superposition of Emotions

In tangled webs, feelings blend,
A spectrum where shadows mend.
Joy and sorrow intertwine,
In each heartbeat, a sacred sign.

Echoes of laughter dance around,
In silence, a deeper sound.
Hope flickers amidst despair,
In the chaos, love lays bare.

Alternatives lie in every glance,
Every tear a second chance.
Between the layers, truths reside,
In this space, we cannot hide.

Moments rich in colors bright,
Reflecting dreams in soft twilight.
Emotions swirl, a timeless ride,
In superpositions, we confide.

The heart holds all that we feel,
In layers, a tapestry surreal.
From joy to pain, the spectrum flows,
An endless dance that softly grows.

Entropy's Embrace

In a world where chaos spins,
Life dances, and laughter begins.
Fragments of memories collide,
In entropy, we find our stride.

Order fades, and tempests rise,
Yet in the storm, hope never dies.
We learn to waltz through the storm,
Finding warmth in the wildest norm.

Time unwinds, the threads unravel,
Paths emerge where none would travel.
From disarray, new forms arise,
In shattered dreams, the spirit flies.

Every ending births a start,
As chaos reshapes the art.
In the mess, connections thread,
From brokenness, love is spread.

Embrace the tangled, fierce embrace,
In entropy, we find our place.
Together we weave, hand in hand,
In the dance of life, we stand.

Love Beyond the Light Barrier

In the cosmos where time stands still,
Love transcends, an endless thrill.
Distances fade and shadows wane,
In this realm, hearts break the chain.

Across the stars, a whisper flies,
Unseen, yet felt, the soul replies.
Through galaxies, our spirits soar,
Beyond the light, forevermore.

Unraveled paths, they intertwine,
In the dark, your hand meets mine.
Through every tear, through every laugh,
In love's embrace, we've found our path.

No obstacles can dim this fire,
In every pulse, a heart's desire.
Boundless dreams, we chase the night,
Together, we are the wondrous light.

Time may stretch beyond our sight,
Yet love remains, a guiding light.
Beyond the barrier, our souls unite,
In the cosmos, we define our flight.

Love's Infinite Spectrum

In every hue our hearts align,
A spectrum bright, so warm, divine.
From crimson blush to azure skies,
Each shade reveals where passion lies.

Through whispered dreams and laughter's song,
Together, where we both belong.
In vibrant tones, our souls entwine,
A canvas bold, our love's design.

In golden rays of morning light,
We chase the dawn, embrace the night.
In every shade, our spirits soar,
Endless colors, forevermore.

In shadows cast and glimmers bright,
We find our way, our hearts alight.
With each new blend, a story spun,
In every hue, we are as one.

Through every storm, through calm and glee,
Our colors shine, eternally.
In love's embrace, we bloom and grow,
A spectrum vast, our hearts aglow.

Reflections in a Multiverse

In every world, a tale unfolds,
In mirrored realms, our fate still holds.
Amongst the stars in cosmic dance,
Our souls collide, a fateful chance.

In parallel paths, our hearts entwined,
Each choice we make, a love defined.
Through tangled time, in echoes clear,
I find your voice, ever so near.

In endless nights and fleeting days,
We seek the light in different ways.
Yet in each life, in every guise,
Your essence shines, I recognize.

Through portals vast and skies unknown,
In every heart, our love is sown.
With every echo, every spark,
We find our way through light and dark.

In realms where fate is yet to play,
Our love endures, come what may.
In every twist, a thread we weave,
In all dimensions, we believe.

Molecular Bonds of Love

In every spark, a bond ignites,
Atoms dance in gentle lights.
Molecules weave our hearts so tight,
In chemistry, we find our flight.

Through every pulse, the rhythms flow,
In synchronicity, we grow.
With every touch, reactions thrive,
In this embrace, we come alive.

In gentle whispers and soft sighs,
Our union builds, beyond the skies.
Each heartbeat flows, a tether grand,
Together, we will always stand.

In swirling forms, we coexist,
A fusion made, too strong to resist.
Through trials faced and tempests tough,
In love's embrace, we've found enough.

As elements shift and years go by,
Our bond remains, a timeless tie.
In every moment, near or far,
We are the light, our shining star.

The Symmetry of Our Connection

In perfect balance, hearts align,
A mirrored soul, so pure, divine.
In every glance, a world we build,
Our love, a force, forever filled.

In echoes soft and rhythms true,
The symmetry of me and you.
Through every curve and gentle line,
In unity, our spirits shine.

Through ups and downs, we find our way,
In harmony, come what may.
With graceful steps, we dance as one,
In every moment, love's begun.

In whispered words and laughter shared,
Our bond grows strong, forever paired.
With courage bold and hearts set free,
In every heartbeat, you are me.

In this grand space, our lives entwined,
A dance of love, so well-defined.
Through every phase, our truth remains,
In symmetry, our love sustains.

Dimensions of Connection

In the silence we find, whispers awake,
Threads of our souls in the dance we make.
Every glance a bridge, built with intent,
Hearts intertwine, a sacred event.

In shadows we trust, secrets unfold,
Moments held dearly, treasures untold.
Like constellations, we chart our way,
Guided by stars, through night into day.

Across the expanse, time bends and sways,
In laughter we gather, in sorrow we stay.
The fabric of life, stitched with our names,
A tapestry rich, in joys and in pains.

Hands reach across, as if to embrace,
The warmth of your spirit, my solace, my grace.
In echoes of memories, we'll always reside,
Dimensions of love, forever our guide.

With each pulse of life, the rhythm so clear,
In every heartbeat, I feel you near.
The universe stretches, yet here we remain,
In the depths of connection, love conquers all pain.

Cosmic Chemistry

Atoms collide in a dance so divine,
Molecules join in a pattern, a line.
In the depths of the void, elements flare,
Creating a bond, a force beyond compare.

Galaxies spin in a cosmic embrace,
Stars ignite brightly, leaving their trace.
In the silence of night, secrets are shared,
The universe listens, our fates are declared.

Quantum entanglements, threads intertwined,
In the fabric of space, all relationships bind.
From stardust we rise, to stardust we fall,
Cosmic chemistry breathes life into all.

Every reaction a story to tell,
In the heart of the cosmos, we echo, we dwell.
Each particle finds what it longs to pursue,
In this dance of creation, I'm drawn into you.

With every heartbeat, the universe sighs,
In the breath of connection, our spirits arise.
A symphony plays through the vastness of space,
Cosmic chemistry, our timeless embrace.

The Gravity of Heartstrings

In the pull of your gaze, my world begins,
The gravity strong, where love never thins.
A force that binds, not seen but so real,
In the dance of the soul, it's what we conceal.

Tidal waves crash, emotions collide,
With each tender look, our truths coincide.
In silence, we speak, no words need to flee,
The gravity of heartstrings, you're tethered to me.

Through the twists of fate, we wander and roam,
Finding our way, together, we're home.
In the orbits we trace, our rhythms align,
We're planets at war, yet perfectly fine.

As we navigate life, with laughter and tears,
The weight of connection transcends all our fears.
With every heartbeat, the universe listens,
In the gravity of love, our essence glistens.

In moonlit reflections, shadows conspire,
Illuminating paths, our souls never tire.
Through distances vast, we remain intertwined,
The gravity of heartstrings, forever enshrined.

Melodies in the Void

In the stillness profound, whispers take flight,
Melodies linger in the depths of the night.
Each note an echo, a story unfolds,
In the emptiness, beauty holds.

Harmonies weave through the fabric of space,
An orchestra thrives in the vastness, a grace.
Every heartbeat a rhythm, soft and profound,
Melodies in the void, are where love is found.

Through shadows we wander, hand in hand,
Tuning our souls to the music so grand.
In symphonies whispered, we find our way,
Through silence and sound, forever we play.

With every refrain, a new dream takes flight,
In the resonance deep, we are wrapped in light.
The void sings a chorus, a lullaby sweet,
Melodies linger, our hearts in repeat.

In the universe vast, with stars as our guide,
We dance through the cosmos, two souls synchronized.
With harmonies woven, our spirits rejoice,
In the music of being, together, we chose.

Milton Keynes UK
Ingram Content Group UK Ltd.
UKHW022006091024
449514UK00007B/73